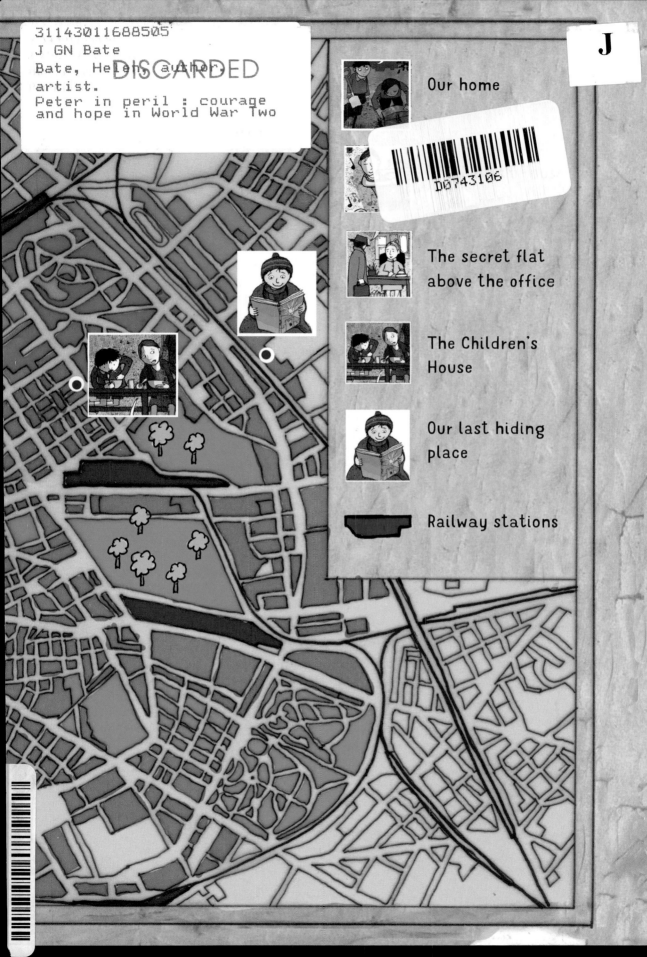

J

D0743106

Our home

The secret flat
above the office

The Children's
House

Our last hiding
place

Railway stations

For Peter's children and grandchildren,
and for all the children in the world
who never make it home.

First published in Great Britain in 2016 by
Otter-Barry Books, Little Orchard, Burley Gate, Herefordshire, HR1 3QS
All rights reserved

A catalogue record for this book is available from the British Library.

ISBN 978-1-91095-957-2

Illustrated with mixed media

Printed in China

9 8 7 6 5 4 3 2 1

# Peter in Peril

## Courage and Hope in World War Two

## Helen Bate

Otter-Barry BOOKS

# My Family Album

Me with Mum and Dad

Me and my cousin Eva

Roza and me

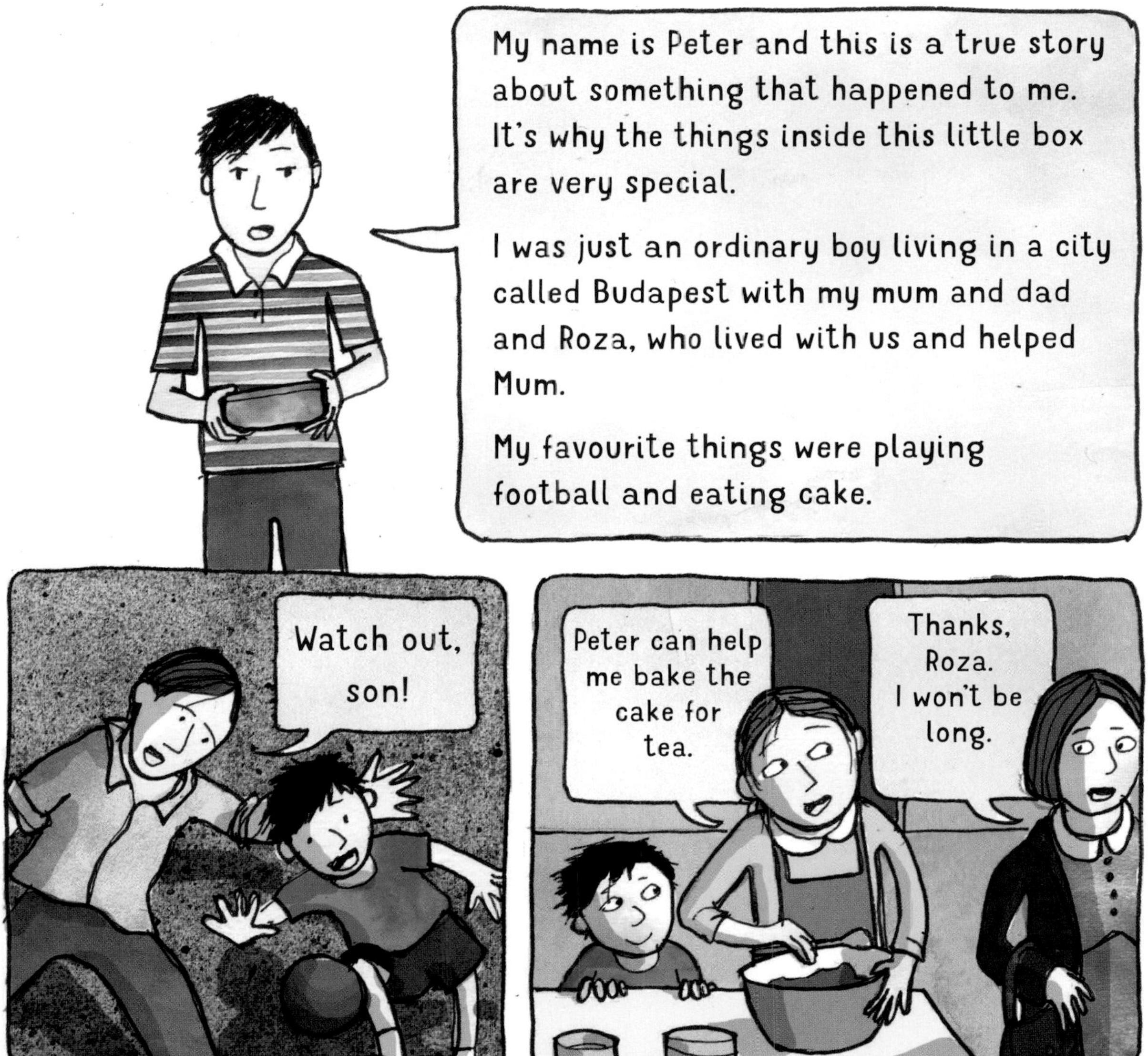
My name is Peter and this is a true story about something that happened to me. It's why the things inside this little box are very special.
I was just an ordinary boy living in a city called Budapest with my mum and dad and Roza, who lived with us and helped Mum.
My favourite things were playing football and eating cake.
Watch out, son!
Peter can help me bake the cake for tea.
Thanks, Roza. I won't be long.
Now I'll leave it to cool, so don't touch it.
She won't notice a bit off the edges.
He'll be in trouble.

In the winter Roza would take me sledging on the hill near our house.
We could see right across the city from up there.

When I was six, I thought the best game in the world was button football.

Me and my cousin Vilmos made all the players out of buttons, but sometimes it got us into a LOT of trouble.

When Mum was angry with me, I'd pack my bag and run away. Roza always came to find me and made me feel better. (Sometimes I wished she was my mum.)

Mum was worried because we were Jewish and new laws made our life very difficult. Roza wasn't allowed to work for us, and she went back to her home in the country.

When she'd gone, I felt like there was a hole where my heart used to be.

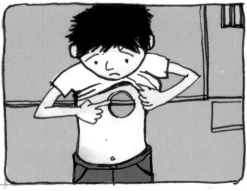

After Roza had gone, my cousin Eva came to live with us. She wanted to stay with her own mum and dad in the country, but they said it wasn't safe there and she should stay with us for a while.

The new rules said all of us Jewish people had to wear big yellow stars on our coats, and we weren't allowed to travel on buses or trains. I thought they were stupid rules!

Then one day, men in uniform came to our house and banged on the door.

They said that we had to leave our home...

and go and live in a different house with lots of other Jewish people. It was really far away and we could only take one bag each.

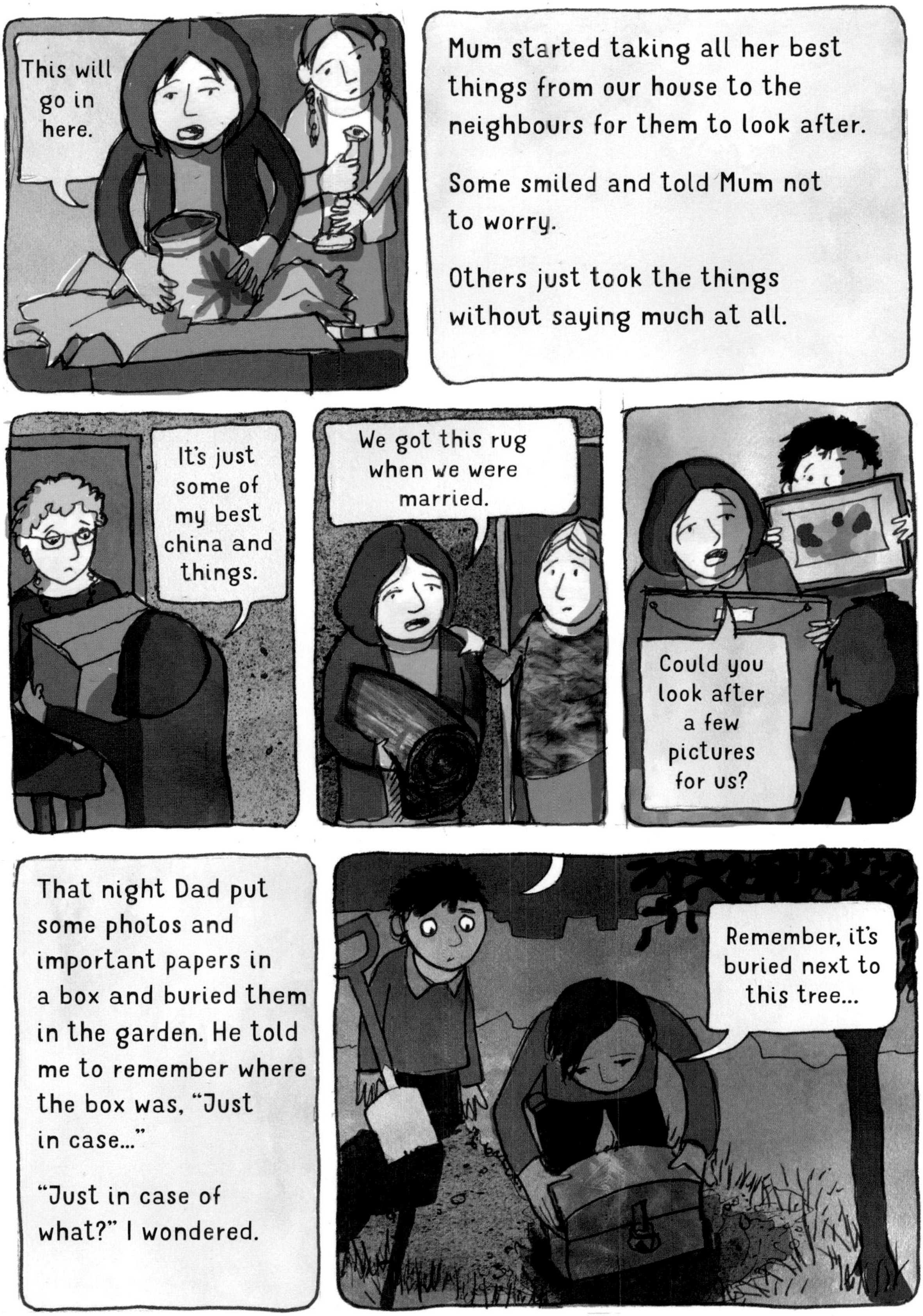
This will go in here.
Mum started taking all her best things from our house to the neighbours for them to look after.
Some smiled and told Mum not to worry.
Others just took the things without saying much at all.
It's just some of my best china and things.
We got this rug when we were married.
Could you look after a few pictures for us?
That night Dad put some photos and important papers in a box and buried them in the garden. He told me to remember where the box was, "Just in case..."
"Just in case of what?" I wondered.
Remember, it's buried next to this tree...

But I don't know what to choose...

The next day we left. Mum said I could take one toy with me so I chose a colouring book and crayons that Roza had given me. I left a few of my best toys for the boy next door to look after. It made me feel really sad.

These won't take up much space.

We walked a long, long way to the new house. We even had to cross the river. Dad said he wouldn't be able to stay with us as he had secret work to do. He said he would see us soon, and we should be brave.

Hurry up, Peter!

Bye, son!

Bye, Dad!

It looks horrid.

We hated this new place. We had one small room to live in, and we had to share a bathroom and kitchen with three other families.

Mum and Eva shared the bed and I had to sleep on a rug on the floor.

I wish Dad was here too.

I know... but we'll be OK.

...and how is your husband?

We were only allowed to go outside for two hours each day, but there were other children to play with, so it wasn't TOO bad. One boy even had a little dog.

Do you want to play with us?

SIT!

Woof!

Eva made friends with a girl who taught her ballet dancing... and they danced for hours!

By now I knew our country was at war. Often at night bombs fell around the city and we all had to shelter in the cellar until the bombing stopped.

I wondered if Dad was sheltering somewhere too.

Sometimes we took the yellow stars off our coats and went to meet Dad in a cafe. He used a secret signal to let us know whether it was safe to talk to him.

There was never enough food so I was always hungry. We all tried not to think about how hungry we were. Sometimes I played button football with my new friends.

At other times I coloured in my colouring book, and then I could almost forget the bad things that had happened.

But one night the house next door was bombed. People came rushing through the wall from the next-door cellar all covered in grey dust.

It was REALLY scary... but not as scary as what happened the next day!

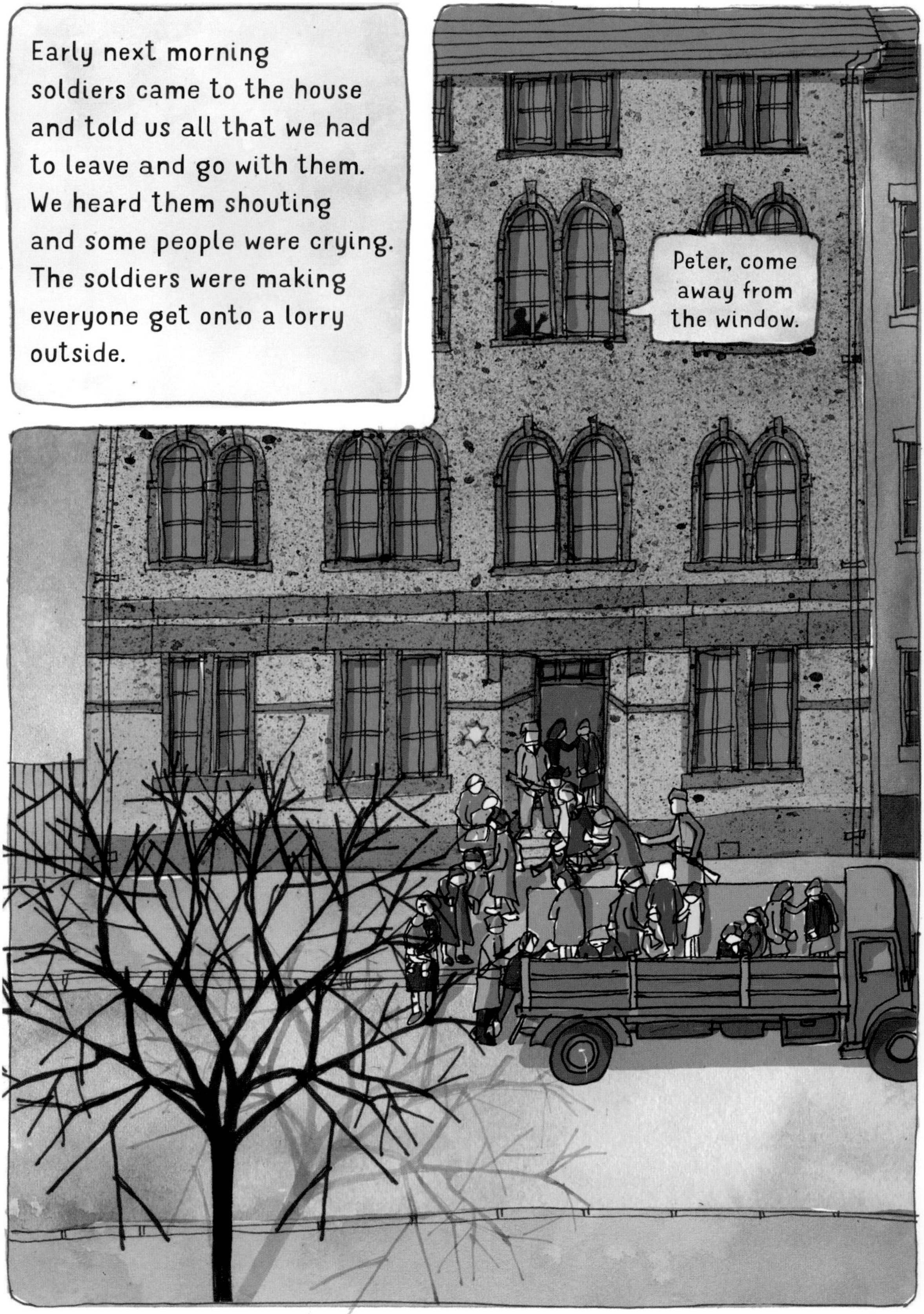
Early next morning soldiers came to the house and told us all that we had to leave and go with them. We heard them shouting and some people were crying. The soldiers were making everyone get onto a lorry outside.
Peter, come away from the window.

We could hear the family from the next room leaving, and we tried to hide in our room.

Then the door burst open and a soldier carrying a gun came in. He said we had to leave too. Mum cried and begged him not to make us go.

The soldier stopped pointing his gun at us and looked towards the door. "Stay here," he said, "but don't make a sound!" Then he left. That night, when it was quiet, we left too.

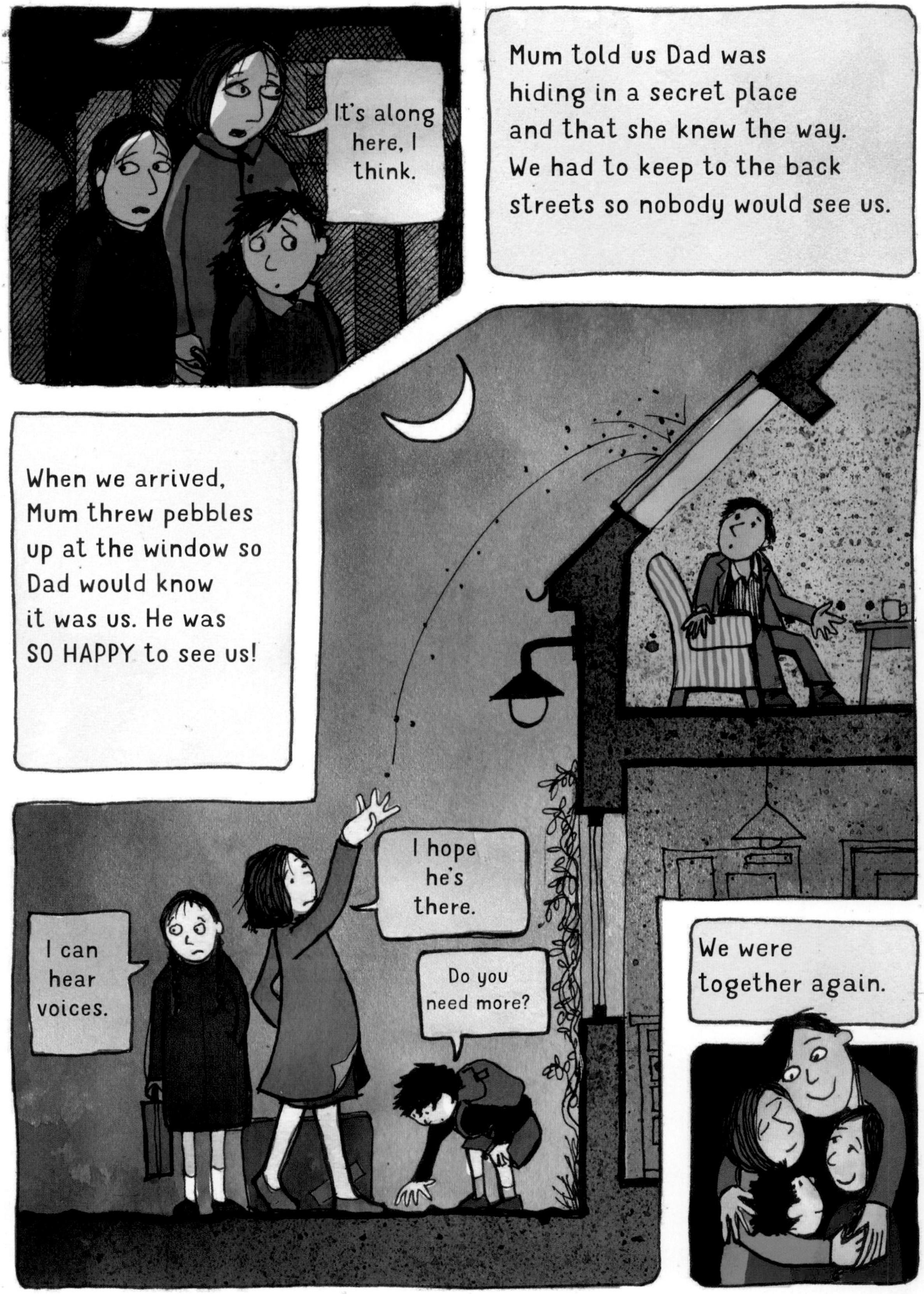
It's along here, I think.
Mum told us Dad was hiding in a secret place and that she knew the way. We had to keep to the back streets so nobody would see us.
When we arrived, Mum threw pebbles up at the window so Dad would know it was us. He was SO HAPPY to see us!
I can hear voices.
I hope he's there.
Do you need more?
We were together again.

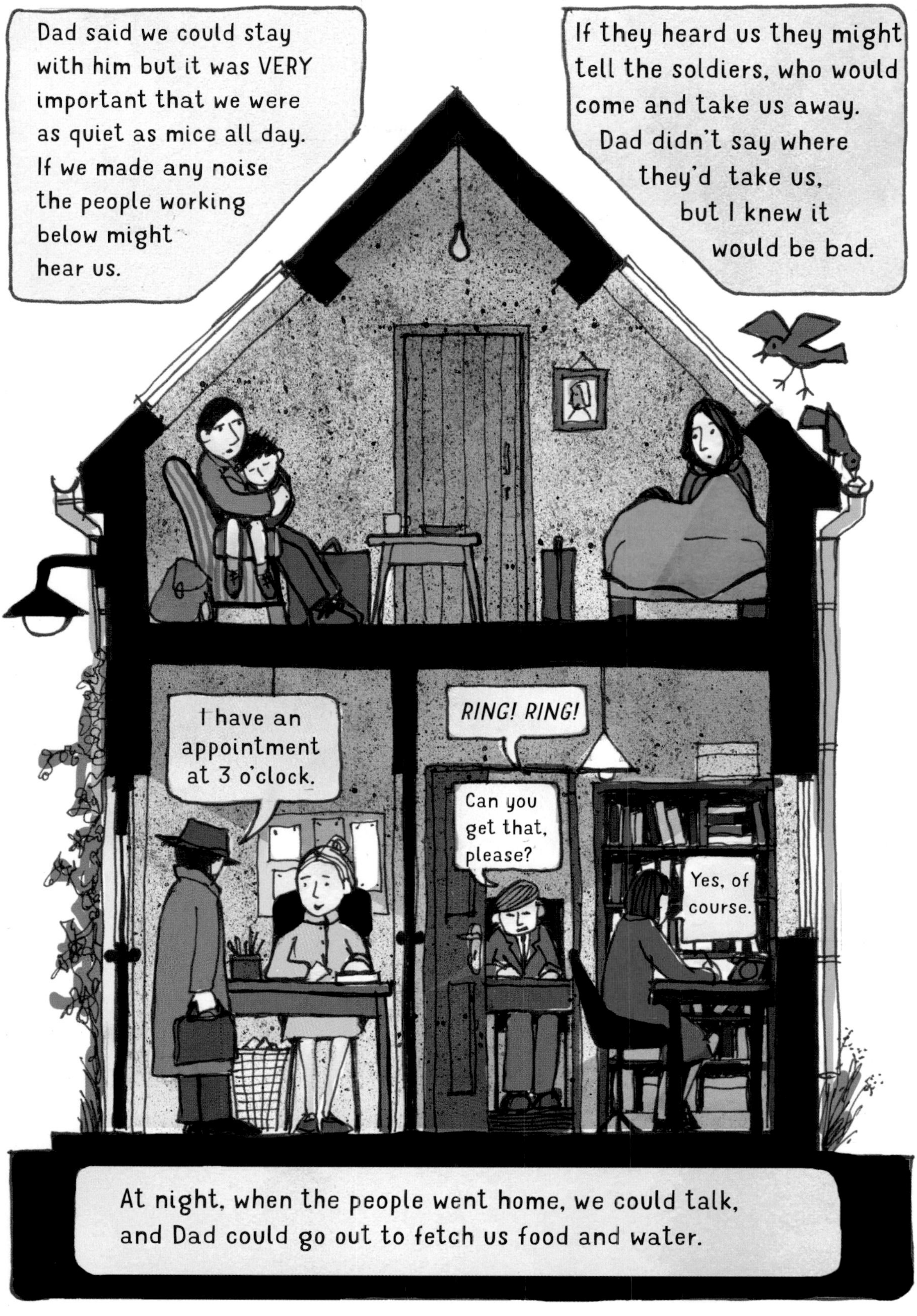
Dad said we could stay with him but it was VERY important that we were as quiet as mice all day. If we made any noise the people working below might hear us.
If they heard us they might tell the soldiers, who would come and take us away. Dad didn't say where they'd take us, but I knew it would be bad.
I have an appointment at 3 o'clock.
RING! RING!
Can you get that, please?
Yes, of course.
At night, when the people went home, we could talk, and Dad could go out to fetch us food and water.

Hiding in a secret place might sound exciting... but actually it was REALLY, REALLY BORING!

It was cold at night and there was nothing to do. There was never enough to eat and I was ALWAYS hungry.

To make us feel better, Dad thought of a guessing game we could play at night, when nobody would hear us.

One night, our game was interrupted when a friend of Dad's came to the secret flat. He had come to tell us about a special Children's House.

He said lots of children were there and we would have a chance to escape with them to a safer country. Mum and Dad were worried, but they decided we should go.

Mum took us to the Children's House and we said goodbye.

Be a good boy.

There were lots of other children there, all without their parents, and a lady who looked after us. I was really worried that we might not see Mum and Dad again.

Don't cry. I'm here.

but they say...

my sister stayed at

my mum says it's just for a while..

We had a meal every day but it was always some sort of noodle soup and it was HORRIBLE! Eva looked after me as if she was my mum, and she scrubbed my face and hands every morning.

Keep still...

Ow... OW!

but Eva, there's hairs in my noodles...

Just EAT it... and be quiet. She'll hear you.

One day, a man who used to work with Dad came to the house. He looked strange dressed in uniform. He told me and Eva that before bedtime we should hide somewhere safe, and not come out until morning. He said it was VERY important that we did what he said.

So that night we hid in a cupboard

and I fell asleep...

SUDDENLY I woke up. There was LOTS of noise. Men shouting in angry voices. Children crying. We were SO scared...

Then there was the sound of a lorry driving away and it was quiet again. Eva said we should leave STRAIGHT AWAY!

The moon was bright outside but we weren't sure where to go. Eva said we would try and find our way back to the secret flat. We hoped and hoped Mum and Dad were still there. We set off walking across the city.

I think it's this way.

It was very, VERY scary and my feet hurt because my shoes were too small.

WOOF! WOOF!

Grrr!

Quick, just keep walking.

We saw a few people, but we made sure they didn't see us.

Most people were asleep...

Eva wasn't sure which was the right way...

I think it's down here.

No... that doesn't look right...

Are we lost?

Look at all the rats, Eva.

and the bombed buildings looked scary in the moonlight. We saw one rat as big as a CAT! Eva was scared and made us go the other way.

Then Eva said she knew where we were and I spotted the secret flat at the end of the street. We ran towards it. Eva threw pebbles up at the roof window to let Mum and Dad know we were there... but nothing happened. What if they had moved? Or been taken away? Eva threw some more... and then...

They MUST be there.

Mum and Dad appeared at the door. I was SO happy to see them.

While Eva and I slept, Mum and Dad decided what to do.

The next morning it was all arranged.

Eva would stay with a kind lady until the war was over...

Dad would carry on his secret work...

and Mum and me would go and stay...

in a new hiding place. It was the most horrible place I have ever lived in and I HATED it!

Mum slept a lot and it was REALLY cold.

I wish Eva was here...

Oh dear! Can you feel that?

It was so cold that I couldn't feel my toes. Mum said it was frostbite and she wrapped my feet in her cardigan.

There was nothing to eat and Mum even had to collect snow to melt for drinking water. My colouring book was full and I'd lost all my crayons.

I'm BORED!

Then, one freezing morning, when I woke up, Mum was smiling.

Happy Birthday, Peter !!

It was my birthday and Mum had somehow got me a present. It was all wrapped up in brown paper.

I tried to guess what it could be. When I took off the wrapping paper I was SO happy!

Do you like it?

A book full of STORIES!

Thanks, Mum!

It's amazing!

I hope one day YOU get a present that's so special.

There were stories of knights and jungles, wild oceans, animals, castles and explorers...

It was like entering a MAGICAL world.

But in the real world there was fierce fighting in the streets. The Russians had entered the city. Everyone hid in the cellars.

We can hide in here...

BANG! BANG! BANG!

Everyone was afraid.

We could hear the gunfire getting closer and closer, and we wondered when the soldiers would find us. Would they rescue us or kill us?

BANG!

BANG!

I might be able to see what's happening.

That's OK.

But you're hurt...

This is a good spider and this is a bad spider...

She sounds very weak.

What can I do?

The fighting went on for a long time. We had to stay in the cellar for WEEKS – and we had hardly any food.

It was very cold and damp and dark, and we didn't sleep well because it was uncomfortable and noisy, with either shooting outside or snoring and babies crying inside.

In the daytime I read the same stories over and over again.

...and the captain called for the men to grab the ropes and haul the whale to the side of the boat, but as they did, the boat...

One day when I was reading the story about a giant whale again, the door to the cellar BURST OPEN!

BANG!

Russian soldiers ran in, pointing their guns at us and shouting!

не двигаться!

оставайтесь на месте!

One made everyone hand over their watches to him...

but the other reached into his pocket, smiled and gave me a chunk of bread.

When the soldiers had gone, everything went quiet. We waited until the others had left and then we went outside. Mum said the fighting must be over.

*Russian translation:* Don't move! Stay where you are!

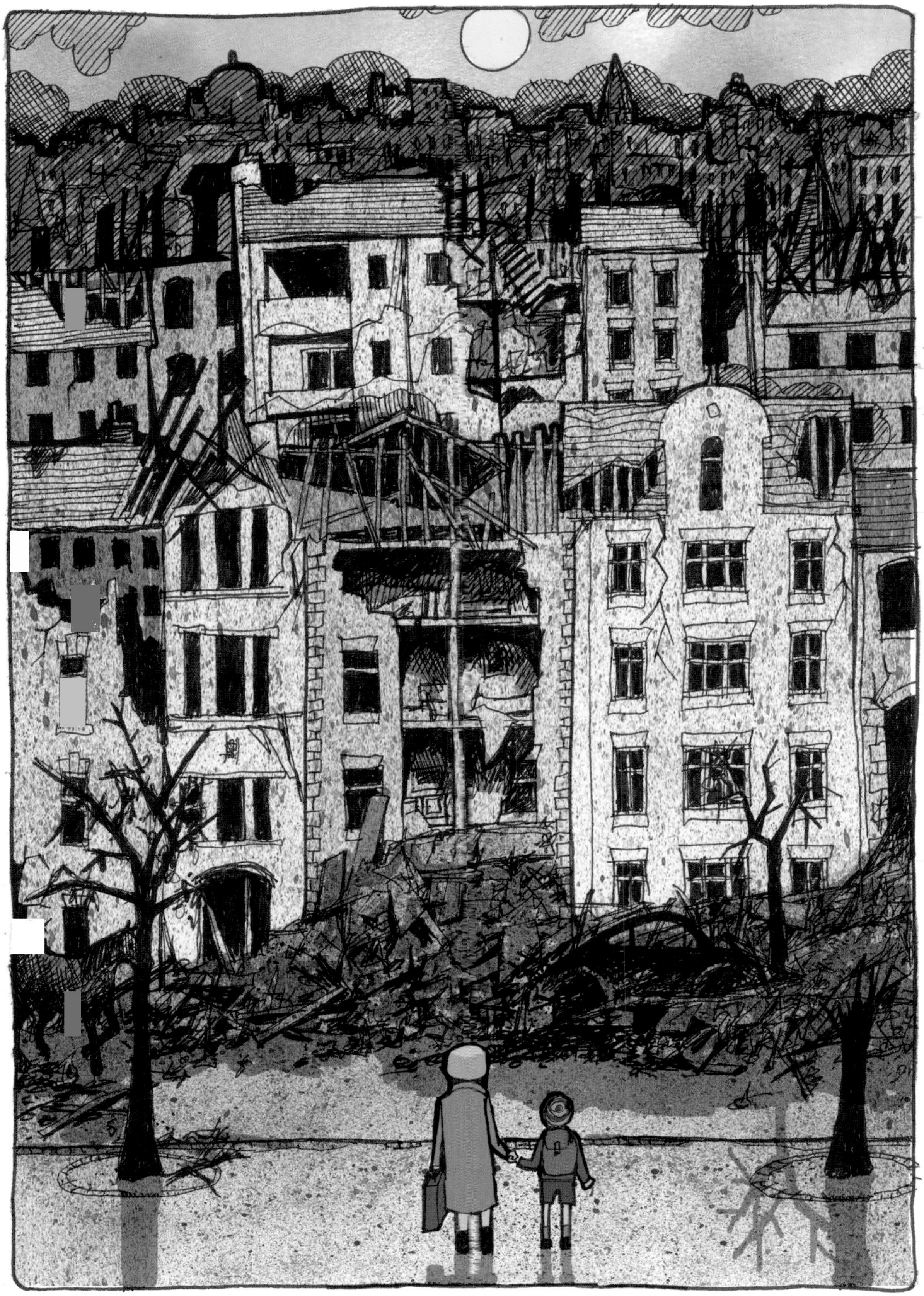

Mum said we should wait and Dad would be sure to come and find us soon...
and then I saw him!

He gave me the BIGGEST hug!

We had to walk all the way home across the ruined city.

...and they stole our watches too...

I wonder if Eva is all right?

My feet REALLY hurt!

The bridges were destroyed but the river was frozen, so we all crossed on the ice. When we got home there was a big hole in the wall and a machine gun in Dad's study...

We're home!

My bedroom was in a mess but we soon started to get everything back to normal again. Our neighbour had looked after some of my toys but I felt a bit too old for them now.

Thanks!

Here's your train set.

It's still here!

Dad dug up the box with our money and important papers and Mum got some of our things back too.

People have been kind.

Eva came back to live with us for good, but there was still not enough food, and we were all still hungry.

I'm afraid that's all there is today.

Mum and Dad were always busy rebuilding our house, so most of the time I went exploring with my friends. There was loads to do in the ruined streets. We found unexploded bullets and emptied out the gunpowder to make trails of fire.

They hissed and burned with a bright flame. Sometimes we burned our fingers by accident. It hurt but we didn't care.

We went fishing in the river with an old sheet and caught lots of fish. I took them home in a bucket and put them in the bath so they'd grow big enough to eat...

So me and Eva were sent on a goods train to stay with Roza in the country.

but Mum wasn't very happy. She said, "He's running WILD!" and, "We'll HAVE to do something!"

Roza was so pleased to see us. She introduced us to her family and said she was going to feed us up. She said I could help with her jobs.

This is Miklos.

Hello.

Cluck!

I collected the eggs and milked the goat...

and I learned to swim in the bottomless lake.

I climbed every tree in the orchard and Eva got a boyfriend with a motorbike. It was fun and I was NEVER hungry.

Shall we go and cool some watermelons in the well again?

One day, I was collecting eggs near an empty house, when I spotted something half hidden in the ground, under a bush.

I scraped away the dry earth with my hands and dug it out. It was an old tin box!

Inside, I found a collection of tin soldiers, all carefully painted in blue and gold, and a note with writing on it. I took it to show Roza. She told me it belonged to a boy called Daniel who had lived in the village. Soldiers had taken him and his family away.

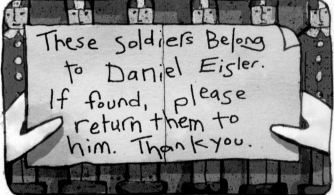

These soldiers belong to Daniel Eisler. If found, please return them to him. Thank you.

Daniel must have hidden these before he left.

You can keep them, Peter. I'm sure Daniel would want you to.

Roza said I should take care of the soldiers, as Daniel might come back one day. I washed them and put them back in the tin box, and hid them under my bed. Then I wrote a note telling Daniel that his soldiers were safe and waiting for him. I put the note in a glass jar under the same bush where I'd found the box. I really hoped he would find it there.

What does it say?

A few days later we were picking apples, when Roza came to tell us that a letter had come from Mum. We were going back home next week!

But the best news was that Roza was coming back to live with us. Mum and Dad were at the railway station to meet us and they were amazed at how much we'd grown. Mum said she had some exciting news.
I was going to have a new brother or sister!

You are both SO BIG!

OW!!

That winter my baby brother Andras was born. He is a real pest! One day I'll tell him the story of the tin soldiers and I'll let him play with them if he's careful. But I'll make sure he remembers that we're only looking after them for Daniel....

# Background to the Story of Peter

This is the true story of Peter and his family, who lived in Hungary's capital city of Budapest during the Second World War (1939-45). They were one of many Jewish families in Hungary. Even before the war, laws were made which restricted their freedom. When Hungary entered the war on the side of Germany, things became even worse for the Jewish community. Their homes were taken away by the government and many were forced to live, all together, in parts of the city that were like prisons.

When the Nazis, who ruled Germany under Adolf Hitler, took control of Hungary in early 1944, a really terrible time began for Hungarian Jews. Hundreds of thousands were taken away to concentration camps, where most of them were killed or died of hunger and disease. This was the Holocaust, Hitler's campaign to destroy the whole Jewish people. Some brave men and women risked their own safety to hide and protect Hungarian Jewish families, while others handed them over to the police.

In early 1945 the Russian army captured Budapest after heavy fighting that went on throughout the freezing winter. Many thousands of people were killed or injured, and more died of starvation, cold and disease. By the time the city was taken by the Russians on 13 February, 1945, it was in ruins, with its people struggling to survive in cellars and wrecked houses.

It took a long time for the city and its people to recover from the terrible effects of the war. Some Jewish children lost all their relatives and rebuilt their lives with new families in other countries. Others, like Peter and Eva, continued to grow up in Hungary after the war.

Many children in other European countries lived through similar experiences during the Second World War. They can never forget the years of fear and sadness that they lived through.

Today, in some countries of the world, children continue to suffer because of war. There will always be wars, but there will also always be an opportunity for good people to make a difference.

In the courtyard of the Great Synagogue of the city of Budapest there is a large, shiny, steel sculpture of a weeping willow tree. Every leaf bears the name of a Jewish person from Hungary who was killed by the Nazis.

## Universal Declaration of Human Rights

As a direct result of the Second World War the Universal Declaration of Human Rights was created and adopted in 1948 by the fifty countries of the United Nations. It tells us we are all born free and equal. Human rights are fundamental rights that uphold freedom, truth, justice and fairness.

# The Real Peter and his Family

This story is based on the recollections of Peter, who was a child in Budapest during World War Two. Peter's cousin, Eva, came to live with Peter and his parents when her own family, who lived in the countryside, felt that she would be safer in Budapest. Soon afterwards she received a message from the headmaster at her old school, that she should not return home as her parents had been taken away by the Nazis. They were killed, along with Peter's grandmother, aunts and uncles, in the concentration camps. After the war Eva lived with Peter, his parents and his new baby brother, Andras.

Roza (whose real name was Erzsi) was a Catholic woman from the countryside who was employed to look after Peter and help with the housework. After the war she returned to work for the family and stayed with them for many years.

Erzsi (Roza) and Peter in 1938

Peter with Eva in 1939

Peter with his mother
and father in 1941

Peter now lives in Austria with his English wife, Margaret. They have two sons, one daughter-in-law and two grandchildren. Peter regularly returns to visit Eva and Andras, who still live in Budapest .

Peter with his sons, Alex and Mark,
and his grandchildren, Chloe and Ben, in 2015

© www.leighbishopphotography.com

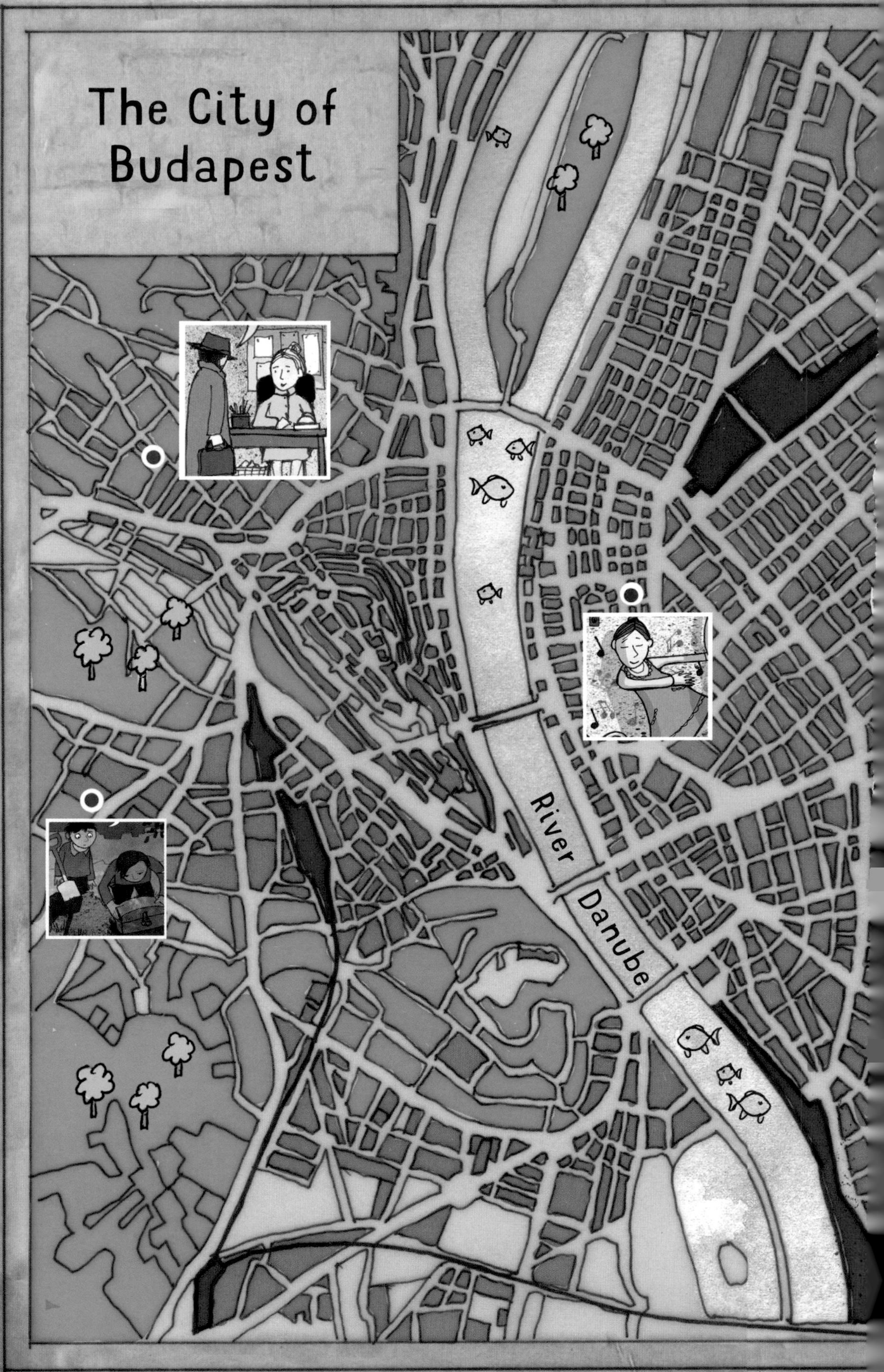

The City of Budapest
River Danube